THE COMPLETE PLANT BASED RENAL DIET COOKBOOK

A Comprehensive Guide on Flexible Recipes that Helps with Managing Kidney Disease and Avoiding Dialysis

By

Gregory Vesely

Copyright © 2023 by Gregory Vesely

DISCLAIMER

The recipes provided in this cookbook are intended for informational purposes only and should not be considered as professional advice. While every effort has been made to ensure the accuracy and reliability of the information and measurements presented, the authors and publishers cannot be held responsible for any errors, omissions, or variations in individual cooking results.

Cooking involves inherent risks, including but not limited to cuts, burns, and allergic reactions. It is important to exercise caution, follow proper food safety guidelines, and use your own judgment when handling ingredients, appliances, and cooking techniques.

Furthermore, please be aware that individual dietary needs and preferences may vary. It is recommended to consult with a qualified healthcare professional or nutritionist regarding any specific dietary concerns or restrictions before incorporating the recipes in this cookbook into your meal planning.

By using this cookbook, you acknowledge and agree that the authors and publishers are not liable for any loss, injury, or damage caused directly or indirectly by the use or misuse of the information presented herein. The responsibility for your cooking endeavors lies solely with you, the reader.

Remember to always cook responsibly, enjoy the process, and savor the delicious results!

To Learn More, You can reach me at gregoryveselykdp@gmail.com for a consultation.

TABLE OF CONTENTS

Other Books by the Author

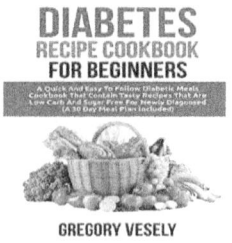

Diabetes Recipes Cookbook for Beginners

Plant-Based Diet Cookbook for Seniors

Pcos Diet Cookbook For Newly Diagnosed

The Complete Prevent And Reverse Heart Disease Cookbook

INTRODUCTION

Sarah lived in a small town nestled among rolling hills. Sarah was a vibrant, compassionate woman who had always enjoyed an active and fulfilling life. However, her journey took an unexpected turn when she was diagnosed with chronic kidney disease. Overwhelmed with emotions and uncertain about her future, Sarah embarked on a quest to regain control of her health. Determined to find a solution, Sarah immersed herself in research and consulted with healthcare professionals specializing in renal health. While searching, she stumbled upon the concept of a plant-based renal diet. Intrigued by the potential benefits, she decided to give it a try.

With newfound enthusiasm, Sarah embarked on a culinary adventure. She discovered the bountiful array of colourful fruits and vegetables, whole grains, legumes, and plant-based protein sources that would become the foundation of her new diet. She learned to create delicious and nourishing meals that satisfied her taste buds and supported her kidney health.

As the weeks turned into months, Sarah noticed remarkable changes within her body. Her energy levels began to rise, and she experienced a renewed sense of vitality. Gone were the days of feeling constantly drained. Sarah's creativity in the kitchen expanded, and she discovered the joy of experimenting with new flavours and ingredients.

Not only did the plant-based renal diet help Sarah regain her vitality, but it also had a positive impact on her overall well-being. She noticed a significant reduction in her blood pressure, a common issue for individuals with kidney disease. Her body weight stabilized, and she felt more confident in her appearance. Moreover, the diet improved her cholesterol levels, reducing her risk of cardiovascular complications.

Sarah's renal function also showed promising signs of improvement. Regular visits to her nephrologist revealed that her kidney function had stabilized and that the progression of her disease had slowed down. Her doctor attributed these positive changes to the nourishing and healing properties of the plant-based diet.

In recent years, there has been growing recognition of the importance of diet in maintaining kidney health and managing renal conditions. One approach that has gained significant attention is the plant-based renal diet, which focuses on incorporating a variety of plant-based foods while limiting the intake of certain nutrients that can be detrimental to kidney function. This dietary approach offers a promising alternative for individuals with kidney disease, providing health benefits while supporting overall well-being.

The renal system is crucial in filtering waste products and excess fluids from the blood, maintaining electrolyte balance, and regulating blood pressure. Diet modification to prevent further damage and manage associated complications becomes essential when the kidneys are impaired. Traditionally, renal diets have emphasized limiting protein, sodium, potassium, and phosphorus intake, often leading to dietary restrictions that can be challenging to adhere to in the long term.

On the other hand, the plant-based renal diet focuses on a predominantly plant-centred approach, incorporating an abundance of fruits, vegetables, whole grains, legumes, nuts, and seeds. This dietary pattern offers several advantages for individuals with kidney disease. Plant-based foods are generally lower in phosphorus and sodium than animal-based products, which helps reduce the kidney burden.

CHAPTER 1

A plant-based renal diet is a dietary approach that emphasizes the consumption of plant-based foods while limiting the intake of certain nutrients that can harm kidney function. This dietary pattern has gained popularity in recent years as a promising alternative for individuals with kidney disease, as it provides numerous health benefits while supporting overall well-being.

The primary focus of the plant-based renal diet is on incorporating a variety of fruits, vegetables, whole grains, legumes, nuts, and seeds. These foods are rich in essential nutrients, such as fibre, vitamins, minerals, and antioxidants, which help support overall health and well-being. In addition, plant-based foods are generally lower in phosphorus and sodium. These two nutrients can be detrimental to kidney function when consumed in excess.

The plant-based renal diet also emphasizes the importance of limiting the intake of certain foods that can harm kidney health. These include animal products, processed foods, and foods high in phosphorus, sodium, and potassium. Animal products, such as meat, dairy, and eggs, are typically high in protein and phosphorus, which can be difficult for the kidneys to process. On the other hand, processed foods are often high in sodium and other additives that can lead to fluid retention and high blood pressure, which can be detrimental to kidney health.

A plant-based renal diet can offer numerous health benefits for individuals with kidney disease. Studies have shown that this dietary approach can help improve blood pressure, reduce inflammation, and slow the progression of kidney disease. In addition, a plant-based diet can help lower the risk of cardiovascular disease, a common complication of kidney disease.

When following a plant-based renal diet, working with a healthcare professional, such as a registered dietitian or a nephrologist, is essential to ensure the diet is tailored to meet individual needs. These professionals can provide guidance on specific nutrient needs, monitor kidney function, and provide support and resources to help individuals adhere to the diet.

A plant-based renal diet is a dietary approach that emphasizes the consumption of plant-based foods while limiting the intake of certain nutrients that can harm kidney function. This dietary pattern can offer numerous health benefits for individuals with kidney disease, supporting overall health and well-being. Working with a healthcare professional is essential when following this diet to ensure it is tailored to meet individual needs and goals.

A plant-based renal diet is a dietary approach that focuses on consuming predominantly plant-based foods while limiting the intake of nutrients that can harm kidney function. This dietary pattern is gaining popularity as a promising alternative for individuals with kidney disease, as it provides numerous health benefits while supporting overall well-being.

The primary goal of the plant-based renal diet is to include a variety of fruits, vegetables, whole grains, legumes, nuts, and seeds in one's diet. These foods are rich in essential nutrients, such as fibre, vitamins, minerals, and antioxidants, which can help support overall health and well-being. Moreover, plant-based foods are generally low in phosphorus and sodium, two nutrients detrimental to kidney function when consumed in excess.

In contrast, the plant-based renal diet encourages limiting or avoiding consuming animal products, processed foods, and foods high in phosphorus, sodium, and potassium. Animal products, such as meat, dairy, and eggs, are often high in protein and phosphorus, which can be difficult for the kidneys to process. On the other hand, processed foods are typically high in sodium and other additives that can lead to fluid retention and high blood pressure, which can be detrimental to kidney health.

By following a plant-based renal diet, individuals can experience numerous health benefits. Studies have shown that this dietary pattern can help improve blood pressure, reduce inflammation, and slow the progression of kidney disease. Moreover, a plant-based diet can help lower the risk of cardiovascular disease, a common complication associated with kidney disease.

It is important to note that the plant-based renal diet should be tailored to meet individual needs, and consultation with a healthcare professional, such as a registered dietitian or a nephrologist, is recommended. These professionals can provide guidance on specific nutrient needs, monitor kidney function, and provide support and resources to help individuals adhere to the diet.

A plant-based renal diet is a dietary approach that emphasizes the consumption of predominantly plant-based foods while limiting the intake of nutrients that can harm kidney function. This dietary pattern can offer numerous health benefits for individuals with kidney disease, supporting overall health and well-being.

The plant-based renal diet offers several benefits for individuals with kidney disease. Here are some of the critical advantages of following this dietary approach:

1. Kidney Function Support: The plant-based renal diet focuses on foods that are generally lower in phosphorus, sodium, and potassium, which can be challenging for the kidneys to process in excessive amounts. By reducing the intake of these nutrients, the diet helps lessen the workload on the kidneys, potentially slowing the progression of kidney disease and preserving kidney function.

2. Blood Pressure Management: High blood pressure is a common complication of kidney disease. The plant-based renal diet, rich in fruits, vegetables, whole grains, and legumes, is naturally low in sodium and high in potassium, fibre, and antioxidants. This combination of nutrients has been shown to help lower blood pressure levels, reducing the risk of cardiovascular issues and further kidney damage.

3. Heart Health Promotion: Individuals with kidney disease often face an increased risk of cardiovascular problems. The plant-based renal diet, emphasizing plant foods and limited intake of saturated and trans fats, cholesterol, and sodium, can help lower cholesterol levels, decrease inflammation, improve blood vessel function, and reduce the risk of heart disease.

4. Nutrient-Rich Diet: The plant-based renal diet encourages a diverse range of plant-based foods, providing a wealth of essential nutrients, including fibre, vitamins (such as C, E, and folate), minerals (such as magnesium and potassium), and antioxidants. These nutrients contribute to overall health, immune system support, and protection against chronic diseases.

5. Weight Management: Obesity and excess weight can worsen kidney disease and increase the risk of related complications. Plant-based foods are typically lower in calories and fibre, promoting a feeling of fullness and making it easier to maintain a healthy weight or achieve weight loss goals. The plant-based renal diet can support weight management efforts when combined with appropriate portion control.

6. Improved Digestive Health: The high fibre content of the plant-based renal diet promotes healthy digestion and can help prevent or alleviate common gastrointestinal issues, such as constipation. Adequate fibre intake supports regular bowel movements, helps remove

waste products efficiently, and may reduce the risk of diverticulosis and other digestive disorders.

7. Enhanced Overall Well-being: Following a plant-based renal diet often leads to an increased intake of natural, unprocessed foods. These foods are typically rich in phytonutrients and antioxidants, associated with numerous health benefits, including reduced inflammation, improved energy levels, enhanced immune function, and a decreased risk of various chronic diseases.

It's important to note that the plant-based renal diet should be personalized to meet individual needs, considering factors such as stage of kidney disease, nutrient levels, and medical history. Working with a healthcare professional, such as a registered dietitian or nephrologist, can help ensure the diet is appropriately adapted and monitored for optimal results.

Foods to Eat and Avoid on the Plant-Based Renal Diet

A plant-based renal diet is a diet that includes more plant foods and fewer animal foods for people with kidney disease. It may help prevent and slow the progression of chronic kidney disease, type 2 diabetes, high blood pressure, and heart disease.

Some foods to eat on a plant-based renal diet are:

- Wholesome grains, exemplified by oats, brown rice, quinoa, and barley.
- Succulent fruits, gracing our palates with the essence of apples, bananas, berries, and oranges.
- Verdant vegetables, adorning our plates with leafy greens, broccoli, carrots, and tomatoes.
- Nutritious nuts, bestowing upon us their goodness in the form of almonds, walnuts, and pistachios.
- Leguminous wonders, comprising beans, peas, and lentils, lending their nourishment to the mix.
- Healthful plant oils, with olive and canola oil being the flag bearers of this league.

Some foods to avoid or limit on a plant-based renal diet are:

- The crimson meats, embodied by beef, pork, and lamb, whisper a cautionary tale.
- Processed meats, donning the guise of bacon, sausage, and ham, beckon us to restrain.
- Dairy products, such as milk, cheese, and yoghurt, may need to be held at bay.
- The ovate treasures that are eggs, though cherished by many, may be restricted.
- Fish and seafood, swimming in culinary temptation, might require temperance.

- Animal fats, clothed in the semblance of butter or lard, may need to take a back seat.

The amount and type of foods you can eat on a plant-based renal diet may vary depending on your kidney function, blood tests, and other health conditions. You should consult with your doctor or dietitian before making any changes to your diet.

CHAPTER 2

Regarding maintaining a renal diet, breakfast is crucial in nourishing and ensuring the well-being of individuals with renal health concerns. A renal diet focuses on managing the intake of certain nutrients, such as sodium, potassium, phosphorus, and protein, to support kidney function and prevent further complications. Designing breakfast recipes that align with the principles of a renal diet is essential for promoting optimal health and reducing the burden on the kidneys.

This guide will explore various considerations and guidelines for creating breakfast recipes suitable for a renal diet. It is important to note that everyone's dietary needs may vary, so it's advisable to consult with a healthcare professional or a registered dietitian who can provide personalized recommendations based on specific medical conditions and individual requirements.

By crafting breakfast recipes tailored to a renal diet, we can ensure a balanced and satisfying start to the day while maintaining the necessary dietary restrictions. From incorporating kidney-friendly ingredients to managing portion sizes, this guide will offer insights to help you make informed decisions when preparing breakfast meals for individuals following a renal diet.

Let's dive into the world of renal-friendly breakfast recipes and discover a variety of options that are not only nutritious but also delicious and enjoyable for those with renal health concerns.

Ingredients

- One moderately sized sweet potato, carefully peeled and cut into small cubes.

- 1 tablespoon olive oil

- 1 small onion, diced

- 2 cloves garlic, minced

- 2 cups fresh spinach leaves

- 4 large eggs

- Salt and pepper to taste

Instructions

1. Warm the olive oil in a frying pan at a moderate temperature.

2. Add the diced sweet potato to the skillet and cook for about 5-7 minutes or until the sweet potato softens.

3. Add the diced onion and minced garlic to the skillet and sauté for 2-3 minutes until the onion becomes translucent.

4. Stir in the fresh spinach leaves and cook until they wilt, approximately 2 minutes.

5. Create four wells in the mixture and crack an egg into each well.

6. Cover the skillet and cook for about 4-5 minutes or until the eggs are cooked to your desired level of doneness.

7. Add a pinch of salt and a dash of pepper according to your preference.

8. Remove the skillet from heat and immediately serve the sweet potato and spinach breakfast skillet.

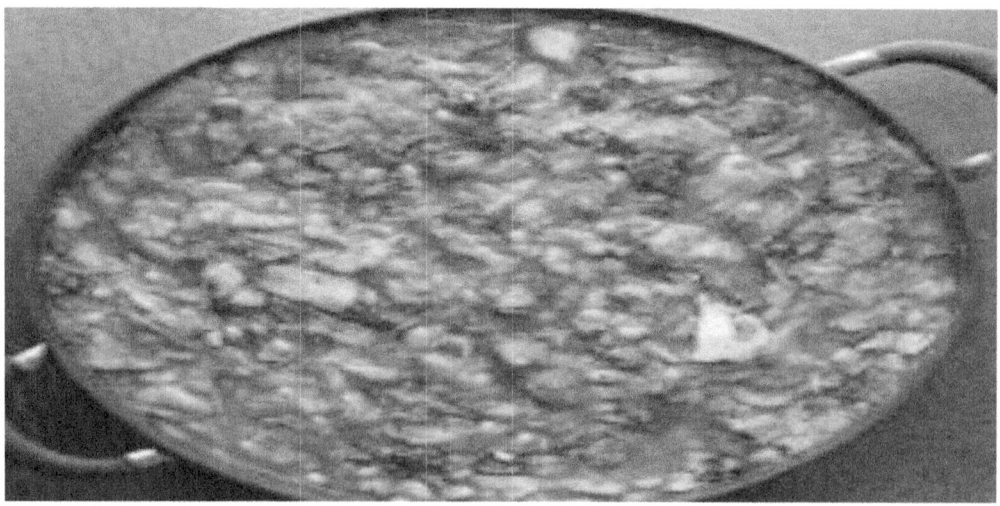

Vegan Blueberry Pancakes

Ingredients

- 1 cup all-purpose flour
- 1 tablespoon baking powder
- 1 tablespoon sugar
- 1/4 teaspoon salt
- One serving of plant-derived milk, such as almond milk or soy milk, measuring approximately 1 cup.
- 1 tablespoon apple cider vinegar
- 1 teaspoon vanilla extract
- 1 cup fresh blueberries
- For lubricating the pan, opt for vegan margarine or a cooking spray.

Instructions

1. Whisk the flour, baking powder, sugar, and salt in a mixing bowl.

2. combine the plant-based milk, apple cider vinegar, and vanilla extract in a separate bowl. Stir well and let it sit for a few minutes to curdle slightly.

3. Pour the wet ingredients into the dry ingredients and whisk until combined. Exercise caution to avoid excessive blending; a handful of clumps are acceptable.

4. Gently fold in the fresh blueberries.

5. Preheat a non-stick pan or griddle over medium heat. Grease the pan with vegan butter or cooking spray.

6. Pour 1/4 cup of the pancake batter onto the pan for each pancake. Continue cooking the mixture until small pockets of air rise and create visible bubbles on the top surface. At that point, carefully turn the mixture over to ensure both sides are evenly cooked and continue cooking until a desirable golden brown color is achieved.

7. Repeat the process with the remaining batter, adding more vegan butter or cooking spray to the pan as needed.

8. Serve the vegan blueberry pancakes warm with maple syrup, additional fresh blueberries, or any desired toppings.

Ingredients

- 1/4 cup chia seeds
- 1 cup plant-based milk (such as almond milk or coconut milk)
- 1 tablespoon maple syrup (or sweetener of your choice)
- 1/2 teaspoon vanilla extract
- Fresh berries (such as strawberries, blueberries, or raspberries) for topping

Instructions

1. Combine the chia seeds, plant-based milk, maple syrup, and vanilla extract in a bowl. Thoroughly blend the ingredients to guarantee uniform dispersion of the chia seeds.

2. Let the mixture sit for about 5 minutes, and then give it another good stir. This will prevent clumping and ensure the chia seeds are well incorporated.

3. Chill the bowl by covering it and placing it in the refrigerator for a minimum of 2 hours or leave it overnight. This will allow the chia seeds to absorb the liquid and create a pudding-like consistency.

4. After the chia seed pudding has set, stir it well to break up any clumps that may have formed.

5. Present the chia seed pudding in individualized bowls or glasses.

6. Tops with fresh berries or other desired toppings, such as sliced almonds or shredded coconut.

7. Enjoy chia seed pudding with berries as a nutritious and satisfying breakfast or snack.

Ingredients

- 1 ripe banana, peeled

- 1 tablespoon almond butter

- 1 cup plant-based milk (such as almond milk or oat milk)

- Consider adding a drizzle of honey or maple syrup (if desired) to introduce a touch of delightful sweetness.

- 1/2 teaspoon vanilla extract

- Optional addition: Ice cubes for an invigoratingly chilled smoothie, if desired.

Instructions

1. In a blender, combine the ripe banana, almond butter, plant-based milk, honey or maple syrup (if using), and vanilla extract.

2. add a few ice cubes to make the smoothie chilled.

3. Combine the various components until they achieve a seamless and luscious consistency.

4. If the smoothie is too thick, add more plant-based milk until you reach your desired consistency.

5. Taste the smoothie and adjust the sweetness by adding more honey or maple syrup if desired.

6. Pour the almond butter and banana smoothie into a glass.

7. Serve it immediately and enjoy!

Tofu Scramble with Veggies

Ingredients

- 1 block of firm tofu

- 1 tablespoon olive oil

- 1/2 onion, diced

- 1 bell pepper, diced

- 1 cup chopped vegetables of your choice (such as spinach, mushrooms, or zucchini)

- 2 cloves garlic, minced

- 1 teaspoon turmeric powder

- 1/2 teaspoon cumin powder

- 1/2 teaspoon paprika

- Salt and pepper to taste

- Optional for embellishment (if desired): Newly harvested botanicals, such as parsley or cilantro.

Instructions

1. Eliminate surplus moisture from the tofu by draining and applying pressure. Disintegrate the tofu into petite fragments either manually or with the aid of a utensil like a fork.

2. On a stovetop pan, warm the olive oil over a moderate flame.

3. Add the diced onion and bell pepper to the skillet and sauté until they soften, about 5 minutes.

4. Stir in the chopped vegetables and minced garlic. Continue cooking for an extra duration of 3 to 4 minutes until the vegetables reach a state of tenderness.

5. Push the vegetables to one side of the skillet and add the crumbled tofu to the other side.

6. Sprinkle the turmeric powder, cumin powder, and paprika over the tofu. Gently stir and combine the tofu with the vegetables.

7. Cook the tofu scramble for 5-7 minutes, stirring occasionally, until the tofu is heated and lightly golden.

8. Season with salt and pepper to taste.

9. Remove the skillet from heat and garnish with fresh herbs, if desired.

10. Serve the tofu scramble with veggies hot as a nutritious and protein-packed breakfast option.

CHAPTER 3

Appetizer and Snack Recipes

Appetizers and snacks are delightful culinary creations that can be enjoyed on various occasions, from casual gatherings to formal events. They serve as enticing preludes to a meal or as delectable bites to satisfy cravings between meals. The options are vast and diverse when selecting appetizer and snack recipes, catering to different tastes and dietary preferences.

This guide will explore a range of appetizer and snack recipes that will please various palates. Whether you're hosting a party, planning a movie night, or simply looking for a tasty treat, these recipes will provide you with inspiration and guidance.

We'll venture into the world of appetizers and snacks without limiting ourselves to a specific list, as endless possibilities exist. From finger foods to dips, from savoury bites to sweet treats, you'll discover a diverse array of easy and enjoyable recipes.

We've got you covered whether you prefer vegetarian, vegan, gluten-free, or other dietary options. You'll find recipes suitable for different dietary restrictions and personal preferences, ensuring everyone can enjoy the joy of appetizers and snacks.

So, let's dive into this culinary exploration and uncover a plethora of delectable appetizer and snack recipes that will impress your guests, tantalize your taste buds, and make any occasion memorable.

Ingredients

For the sweet potato fries:

- 2 medium sweet potatoes

- 2 tablespoons olive oil

- 1/2 teaspoon paprika

- 1/2 teaspoon garlic powder

- 1/4 teaspoon salt

- 1/4 teaspoon black pepper

For the cilantro lime dip:

- 1/2 cup Greek yoghurt (or dairy-free yoghurt for a vegan option)

- 2 tablespoons fresh cilantro, chopped

- 1 tablespoon lime juice

- 1/2 teaspoon lime zest

- 1/4 teaspoon garlic powder

- Salt and pepper to taste

Instructions

1. Preheat your oven to 425°F (220°C) and line a baking sheet with parchment paper.

2. Wash and scrub the sweet potatoes thoroughly. Cut them into thin strips resembling fries.

3. toss the sweet potato strips with olive oil, paprika, garlic powder, salt, and black pepper until well coated in a large bowl.

4. Place the appropriately seasoned sweet potato fries in a solitary formation on the prepped baking tray.

5. Bake for 25-30 minutes, flipping the fries halfway through until they are crispy and golden brown.

6. Prepare the cilantro lime dip While baking the sweet potato fries. In a small bowl, combine Greek yoghurt, chopped cilantro, lime juice, zest, garlic powder, salt, and pepper. Stir until well mixed.

7. Remove the baked sweet potato fries from the oven and let them cool slightly.

8. Serve the sweet potato fries warmly with the cilantro lime dip.

9. Enjoy the delicious combination of crispy sweet potato fries and tangy, creamy cilantro lime dip as a delightful appetizer or snack.

Ingredients

- 1 can (15 ounces) chickpeas, drained and rinsed
- 1 ripe avocado, peeled and pitted
- 2 tablespoons lemon juice
- 2 tablespoons tahini
- 1 clove garlic, minced
- 1/2 teaspoon cumin
- 1/4 teaspoon paprika
- Salt and pepper to taste
- Optional toppings: chopped fresh parsley, a drizzle of olive oil

Instructions

1. combine chickpeas, avocado, lemon juice, tahini, minced garlic, cumin, paprika, salt, and pepper in a food processor or blender.

2. Process the ingredients until smooth and creamy, scraping down the sides as needed. To achieve the preferred texture, incorporate a tablespoon of water if the blend appears excessively dense.

3. Taste the dip and adjust the seasonings if needed, adding more lemon juice, salt, or spices according to your preference.

4. Transfer the chickpea and avocado dip to a serving bowl.

5. garnish the dip with chopped fresh parsley and a drizzle of olive oil if desired.

6. Serve the dip with fresh vegetables, pita bread, or tortilla chips.

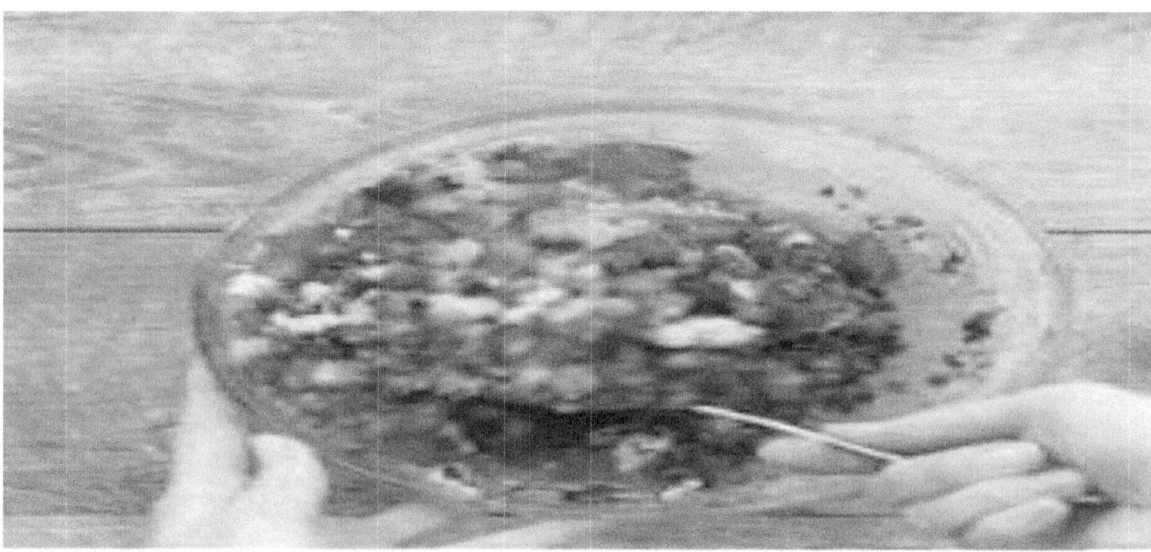

Vegan Buffalo Cauliflower Wings

Ingredients

For the cauliflower wings

- A generously sized cauliflower, meticulously divided into compact florets perfect for bite-sized indulgence.
- 3/4 cup all-purpose flour
- 3/4 cup plant-based milk (such as almond milk or soy milk)
- 1 teaspoon garlic powder
- 1 teaspoon paprika
- 1/2 teaspoon onion powder
- 1/4 teaspoon salt
- 1/4 teaspoon black pepper

For the buffalo sauce

- A quarter-cup of fiery condiment (like Frank's RedHot or Sriracha).
- 2 tablespoons melted vegan butter
- 1 tablespoon maple syrup or agave syrup
- 1 teaspoon apple cider vinegar
- Optional toppings: chopped fresh parsley, celery sticks, vegan ranch or blue cheese dressing for dipping

Instructions

1. In advance, warm up your oven to a temperature of 450 degrees Fahrenheit (230 degrees Celsius) and cover a baking sheet with parchment paper.

2. combine the all-purpose flour, plant-based milk, garlic powder, paprika, onion powder, salt, and black pepper in a large mixing bowl. Stir until smooth and well combined.

3. Dip each cauliflower floret into the batter, coating it evenly, and then place it on the prepared baking sheet. Repeat with all the florets.

4. Bake the cauliflower wings for 20-25 minutes or until they are crispy and golden brown.

5. While the cauliflower wings are baking, prepare the buffalo sauce. In a separate bowl, whisk together the hot sauce, melted vegan butter, maple syrup or agave syrup, and apple cider vinegar until well combined.

6. Once the cauliflower wings are cooked, transfer them to a large mixing bowl.

7. Pour the buffalo sauce over the cauliflower wings and gently toss until evenly coated.

8. Return the coated cauliflower wings to the baking sheet and bake for 10 minutes to allow the sauce to soak in and the wings to become more tender.

9. Remove the cauliflower wings from the oven and let them cool slightly.

10. Serve the vegan buffalo cauliflower wings with optional toppings like chopped fresh parsley, celery sticks, and vegan ranch or blue cheese dressing for dipping.

Raw Vegetable Spring Rolls with Peanut Dipping Sauce

Ingredients

For the spring rolls

- Rice paper wrappers

- Assorted raw vegetables (such as carrots, cucumbers, bell peppers, lettuce, and sprouts)

- Fresh herbs (such as cilantro, mint, or basil), optional

- Rice noodles, cooked according to package instructions, optional

For the peanut dipping sauce

- 1/4 cup peanut butter

- 2 tablespoons soy sauce (or tamari for a gluten-free option)

- spoonful of agave or maple syrup

- 1 tablespoon lime juice

- 1 clove garlic, minced

- 1/2 teaspoon grated ginger

- 2-3 tablespoons water to thin the sauce as needed

Instructions

1. Prepare all the vegetables by washing, peeling, and thinly slicing them into matchstick-like strips.

2. Fill a shallow dish or large plate with warm water.

3. Dip one rice paper wrapper into the warm water and rotate it gently until it softens. This should take about 15-20 seconds.

4. Carefully transfer the softened rice paper wrapper onto a clean surface, such as a cutting board or plate.

5. Place a small handful of rice noodles (if using) on the bottom third of the rice paper wrapper, leaving some space at the edges.

6. Layer a few strips of each vegetable and fresh herbs (if desired) on the rice noodles.

7. Fold the bottom edge of the rice paper wrapper over the filling, then fold in the sides, and roll it tightly to form a spring roll. Continue in the same manner with the remaining ingredients.

8. To make the peanut dipping sauce, mix the peanut butter, soy sauce, maple syrup or agave syrup, lime juice, minced garlic, and grated ginger in a small bowl. Add water, a tablespoon at a time, until the sauce reaches your desired consistency. The sauce ought to be easily pourable and silky.

9. Serve the raw vegetable spring rolls with the peanut dipping sauce on the side.

10. Dip the spring rolls into the sauce and enjoy this refreshing and healthy appetizer or snack.

Ingredients

- 1 can (15 ounces) washed and drained chickpeas

- 1/2 cup dried and drained roasted red peppers

- 3 tablespoons tahini

- 3 tablespoons lemon juice

- 2 tablespoons olive oil

- 1 clove garlic, minced

- 1/2 teaspoon cumin

- 1/2 teaspoon paprika

- Salt and pepper to taste

- Optional toppings: drizzle of olive oil, a sprinkle of paprika, chopped fresh parsley

Instructions

1. combine chickpeas, roasted red peppers, tahini, lemon juice, olive oil, minced garlic, cumin, paprika, salt, and pepper in a food processor or blender.

2. Process the ingredients until smooth and creamy, scraping down the sides as needed.

3. Taste the hummus and adjust the seasonings if needed, adding more lemon juice, salt, or spices according to your preference.

4. If the hummus is too thick, add a tablespoon of water at a time and blend until you reach your desired consistency.

5. Place the hummus with roasted red peppers in a serving bowl.

6. drizzle olive oil on top and sprinkle with paprika for added flavour and presentation.

7. Garnish with chopped fresh parsley for a desired pop of colour.

8. Serve the roasted red pepper hummus with pita bread, fresh vegetables, or crackers.

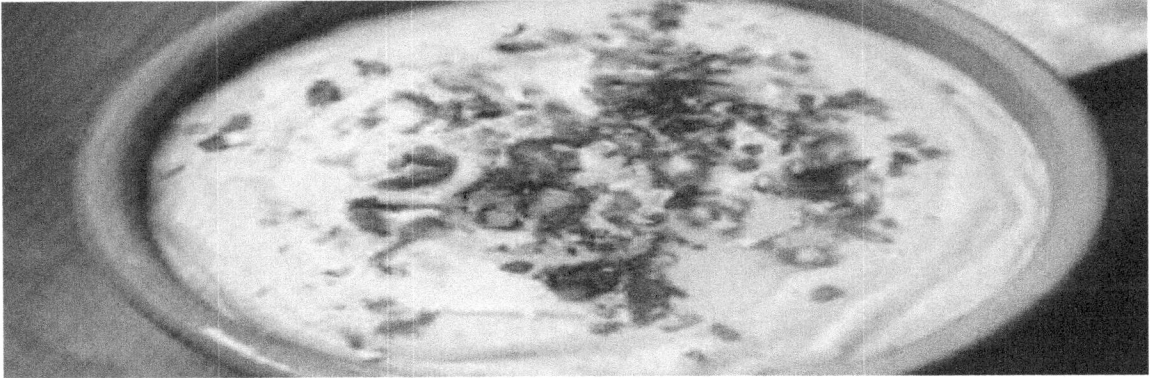

CHAPTER 4

Salads are not only refreshing and nutritious, but they also offer endless possibilities for culinary creativity. Salads can suit your taste preferences and dietary needs, whether you're looking for a light lunch, a side dish, or a complete meal. Regarding a renal diet, incorporating salads can provide various benefits, including managing kidney health and promoting overall well-being.

This section will explore a range of salad recipes suitable for a renal diet. These recipes are designed to be kidney-friendly, considering the restrictions on specific nutrients such as sodium, potassium, and phosphorus. We can create delicious salads that support kidney health by incorporating fresh and wholesome ingredients.

Our selection of salad recipes will include diverse flavours, textures, and ingredients. From crisp greens to colourful vegetables, from lean protein sources to satisfying grains, these salads balance nutrients while satisfying your taste buds. We will also include flavorful dressings and vinaigrettes that enhance the taste and nutritional value of the salads.

Whether managing kidney disease or simply looking to maintain a healthy renal diet, these salad recipes will be a valuable resource. They will inspire you to create vibrant and nourishing salads supporting your well-being. So, let's embark on this journey of exploring renal-friendly salad recipes that will bring joy and wellness to your table.

Ingredients

- 2 medium-sized beets, roasted and peeled
- 2 oranges, peeled and segmented
- 1/4 cup of roasted, roughly chopped walnuts
- 4 cups mixed salad greens
- 2 tablespoons extra-virgin olive oil
- 1 tablespoon balsamic vinegar
- Salt and pepper to taste

Instructions

1. Preheat your oven to 400°F (200°C). Wrap the beets individually in aluminium foil and place them on a baking sheet. Roast for about 40-50 minutes or until the beets are tender when pierced with a fork. Remove from the oven and let them cool.

2. Once the roasted beets have cooled, peel off the skin and cut them into bite-sized cubes.

3. combine the roasted beet cubes, orange segments, and mixed salad greens in a large bowl.

4. In a small bowl, whisk the extra-virgin olive oil, balsamic vinegar, salt, and pepper to create the dressing.

5. Drizzle the dressing over the salad and gently toss to combine, ensuring all the ingredients are coated.

6. Sprinkle the toasted walnuts over the salad for added crunch and flavour.

7. Immediately, Serve the roasted beet and orange salad and enjoy the sweet, earthy, and tangy flavours.

Quinoa and kale salad

Ingredients

- 1 cup quinoa

- 2 cups water or vegetable broth

- 4 cups kale, stems removed and leaves thinly sliced

- 1/2 cup dried cranberries

- 1/2 cup almonds, sliced or slivered

- 1/4 cup red onion, finely chopped

- 2 tablespoons lemon juice

- 2 tablespoons extra-virgin olive oil

- 1 tablespoon maple syrup or honey

- Salt and pepper to taste

Instructions

1. Rinse the quinoa under cold water using a fine-mesh strainer to remove bitterness.
2. bring the water or vegetable broth to a boil in a saucepan. Turn down the heat to low before adding the rinsed quinoa. Cover and simmer for 15-20 minutes until the quinoa is cooked and the liquid is absorbed. Take them out of the oven, then let them cool.
3. combine the cooked quinoa, sliced kale, dried cranberries, sliced almonds, and chopped red onion in a large mixing bowl.
4. whisk together the lemon juice, extra-virgin olive oil, maple syrup or honey, salt, and pepper to create the dressing in a separate small bowl.
5. Drizzle the dressing over the quinoa and kale mixture. Toss well to ensure all the ingredients are coated.
6. Allow the salad 15 minutes to let the flavours meld together and for the kale to soften slightly.
7. Adjust the seasoning and serve the quinoa and kale salad chilled or at room temperature.

Ingredients

- 2 cucumbers, peeled and thinly sliced

- 2 cups cherry tomatoes, halved

- 1/4 cup red onion, thinly sliced

- 2 tablespoons fresh dill, chopped

- Juice of 1 lemon

- 3 tablespoons extra-virgin olive oil

- Salt and pepper to taste

Instructions

1. combine the sliced cucumbers, halved cherry tomatoes, and red onion in a large salad bowl.

2. mix the lemon juice, extra-virgin olive oil, chopped dill, salt, and pepper in a small bowl to create the dressing.

3. Pour the dressing over the cucumber and tomato mixture.

4. Toss well to ensure all the ingredients are coated with the dressing.

5. Let the salad sit for about 10 minutes to allow the flavours to blend and the vegetables to marinate.

6. Taste and adjust the seasoning if needed.

7. Serve the cucumber and tomato salad as a refreshing side dish or a light and healthy standalone salad.

Ingredients

- 2 ripe peaches, halved and pitted

- 4 cups arugula

- 1/2 cup crumbled feta cheese

- 1/4 cup chopped walnuts

- 2 tablespoons balsamic glaze

- 2 tablespoons extra-virgin olive oil

- Salt and pepper to taste

Instructions

1. Preheat a grill or grill pan over medium heat.
2. Lightly brush the peach halves with olive oil.
3. Place the peaches on the grill, cut side down, and cook for about 2-3 minutes until grill marks appear and the peaches soften slightly. Flip the peaches and grill for another 2-3 minutes.
4. Remove the grilled peaches from the heat and let them cool for a few minutes. Once cooled, slice them into wedges.
5. combine the arugula, grilled peach slices, crumbled feta cheese, and chopped walnuts in a large salad bowl.
6. In a small bowl, whisk together the balsamic glaze, extra-virgin olive oil, salt, and pepper to create the dressing.
7. Drizzle the dressing over the salad and toss gently to combine all the ingredients.
8. Serve the grilled peach and arugula salad immediately, enjoying the balance of sweet and savoury flavours.

Ingredients

- 1 cup bulgur wheat

- 1 cup boiling water

- 1 can (15 ounces) of rinsed and drained chickpeas

- 1 cup cucumber, diced

- 1 cup cherry tomatoes, halved

- 1/2 cup red onion, finely chopped

- 1/2 cup fresh parsley, finely chopped

- 14 cup coarsely chopped fresh mint leaves

- Juice of 2 lemons

- 3 tablespoons extra-virgin olive oil

- Salt and pepper to taste

Instructions

1. Place the bulgur wheat in a heatproof bowl and pour the boiling water over it. Cover the bowl with a plate or plastic wrap and let it sit for about 20 minutes, or until the bulgur wheat has absorbed the water and becomes tender. Drain any excess liquid if needed.

2. combine the cooked bulgur wheat, chickpeas, diced cucumber, halved cherry tomatoes, finely chopped red onion, parsley, and mint leaves in a large salad bowl.

3. In a separate small bowl, whisk together the lemon juice, extra-virgin olive oil, salt, and pepper to create the dressing.

4. Drizzle the dressing over the tabbouleh salad mixture and toss well to ensure all the ingredients are coated.

5. Allow the salad to sit for at least 15 minutes to let the flavours meld together and for the bulgur wheat to absorb the dressing.

6. If necessary, taste and adjust the seasoning.

7. Serve the tabbouleh salad with chickpeas as a refreshing and nutritious dish, perfect for lunches, picnics, or as a side dish to complement your main meal.

CHAPTER 5

Maintaining a renal diet means maintaining consistency and variety in main dishes. With a few modifications and thoughtful ingredient choices, you can create delicious and kidney-friendly meals that support your overall well-being. In this guide, we will explore a collection of main dish recipes specifically tailored to the needs of a renal diet.

Regarding a renal diet, it's essential to be mindful of certain nutrients, such as sodium, potassium, and phosphorus. These recipes will focus on incorporating fresh and wholesome ingredients while considering these considerations. By choosing lean proteins, incorporating low-phosphorus grains and vegetables, and using flavorful herbs and spices to enhance the taste, we can create main dishes that are both nutritious and satisfying.

From flavorful baked fish to succulent grilled chicken, from vegetable-based stir-fries to hearty bean stews, these main dish recipes offer a wide range of options to suit different tastes and dietary requirements. They are designed to provide essential nutrients while being mindful of the restrictions of a renal diet.

In addition to being kidney-friendly, these main dish recipes aim to balance flavours, textures, and nutrients to ensure a satisfying dining experience. You'll find recipes that feature a variety of proteins, whole grains, and an abundance of vegetables to create well-rounded meals.

By following these renal-friendly main dish recipes, you can enjoy a diverse and flavorful menu while caring for your kidney health. Whether managing kidney disease or simply seeking a healthier lifestyle, these recipes will help you create nourishing and delicious meals that support your well-being. So, let's dive into the world of kidney-friendly main dish recipes and discover new culinary delights that are both satisfying and beneficial for your renal diet.

Ingredients

- 2 medium zucchinis
- Green or brown lentils, dry, one cup
- 1 tablespoon olive oil
- 1 small onion, finely chopped
- 2 cloves garlic, minced
- 1 carrot, finely chopped
- 1 celery stalk, finely chopped
- 1 can (14 ounces) crushed tomatoes
- 1 teaspoon dried oregano
- 1 teaspoon dried basil
- 1/2 teaspoon dried thyme
- Salt and pepper to taste
- Fresh basil leaves for garnish (optional)

Instructions

1. Trim the ends of the zucchini and use a spiralizer or julienne peeler to create zucchini noodles. Set aside.
2. Rinse the lentils under cold water and cook them according to the package instructions until tender. Drain and set aside.
3. In a big skillet, warm the olive oil over medium heat. The chopped onion should be added and sautéed until transparent.

4. Add the minced garlic, chopped carrot, and celery to the skillet. Cook for another 2-3 minutes, until the vegetables have softened.
5. Add the crushed tomatoes, dried oregano, dried basil, dried thyme, salt, and pepper to the skillet. Stir well to combine.
6. Bring the sauce to a simmer and cook for 15-20 minutes, allowing the flavours to meld together.
7. Add the cooked lentils to the sauce and stir until they are evenly coated.
8. In a separate non-stick pan, lightly sauté the zucchini noodles over medium heat for 2-3 minutes until warm.
9. Serve the zucchini noodles topped with the lentil Bolognese sauce. Garnish with fresh basil leaves if desired.

Mushroom and Lentil Shepherd's Pie

Ingredients

For the filling

- a one cup of dried green or brown lentils

- 3 cups vegetable broth

- 2 tablespoons olive oil

- 1 onion, chopped

- 2 cloves garlic, minced

- 8 ounces mushrooms, sliced

- 1 carrot, diced

- 1 celery stalk, diced

- 1 teaspoon dried thyme

- 1 teaspoon dried rosemary

- Salt and pepper to taste

- 2 tablespoons tomato paste

- 1 tablespoon soy sauce or tamari

- 1 cup frozen peas

For the mashed potato topping

- 4 medium potatoes, peeled and cubed

- 1/4 cup unsweetened plant-based milk

- 2 tablespoons of olive oil or vegan butter

- Salt and pepper to taste

Instructions

1. Preheat the oven to 375°F (190°C).

2. Rinse the lentils under cold water. Lentils and vegetable broth should be mixed together in a pot. After bringing to a boil, lower the heat to a simmer. Cook the lentils for about 20-25 minutes or until tender. Drain any extra liquid, then reserve it.

3. heat the olive oil over medium heat in a large skillet. Add the chopped onion, minced garlic, and sauté until the onion becomes translucent.

4. Include the celery, carrots, and mushroom slices in the skillet. Cook the vegetables for about 5 minutes, or until they are tender.

5. Add the salt, pepper, rosemary, and dry thyme. For the flavors to come out, cook for a further 2 minutes.

6. Add the tomato paste and soy sauce to the skillet. Mix well to coat the vegetables.

7. Add the cooked lentils and frozen peas to the skillet. Stir until everything is well combined. Cook for an additional 2-3 minutes. Remove from heat.

8. In a separate pot, boil the cubed potatoes until they are fork-tender. Potatoes are drained and added back to the saucepan.

9. Mash the potatoes using a potato masher or a fork. Add plant-based milk and vegan butter or olive oil. Add salt and pepper, then continue mashing until the mixture is smooth and creamy.10. Transfer the lentil and vegetable mixture to a baking dish. Spread the mashed potatoes evenly over the top.

11. Place the baking dish in the oven and bake for 25-30 minutes or until the mashed potatoes turn golden brown.

12. Remove from the oven and let it cool slightly before serving.

13. Serve the mushroom and lentil Shepherd's Pie as a comforting and flavorful main dish.

One-Pot Vegetable and Quinoa Stew

Ingredients

- 1 tablespoon olive oil
- 1 onion, chopped
- 2 cloves garlic, minced
- 1 carrot, diced
- 1 celery stalk, diced
- 1 bell pepper, diced
- 1 zucchini, diced
- 1 cup diced tomatoes (fresh or canned)
- 1 cup chopped kale or spinach
- 1 cup quinoa, rinsed
- 4 cups vegetable broth
- 1 teaspoon dried thyme
- 1 teaspoon dried oregano
- Salt and pepper to taste
- Fresh parsley for garnish (optional)

Instructions

1. In a large pot, warm the olive oil over medium heat. Add the chopped onion, minced garlic, and sauté until the onion becomes translucent.

2. Add the diced carrot, celery, bell pepper, and zucchini to the pot. Cook for about 5 minutes, until the vegetables begin to soften.

3. Stir in the diced tomatoes and chopped kale or spinach. Cook for another 2 minutes, until the kale or spinach wilts slightly.

4. Add the rinsed quinoa to the pot, followed by the vegetable broth, dried thyme, oregano, salt, and pepper. Stir well to combine.

5. After bringing the mixture to a boil, turn down the heat. Cover the pot and let the stew simmer for about 20-25 minutes, or until the quinoa is cooked and the vegetables are tender.

6. If necessary, taste and adjust the seasoning..

7. Ladle the vegetable and quinoa stew into bowls and garnish with fresh parsley if desired.

8. Serve the one-pot vegetable and quinoa stew as a hearty and nourishing main dish.

Ingredients

- 4 large Portobello mushrooms
- 2 tablespoons olive oil
- 1 small onion, finely chopped
- 2 cloves garlic, minced
- 2 cups fresh spinach, chopped
- 1/2 cup cashews, finely chopped
- 1/4 cup grated Parmesan cheese (optional)
- Salt and pepper to taste
- Fresh parsley for garnish (optional)

Instructions

1. Preheat the oven to 375°F (190°C). Use parchment paper to line a baking sheet..

2. Clean the Portobello mushrooms by gently wiping them with a damp cloth. Trim the stems off and reserve them.

3. Place the mushroom caps on the prepared baking sheet, gill-side up.

4. heat one tablespoon of olive oil over medium heat in a skillet. Add the chopped onion, minced garlic, and sauté until the onion becomes translucent.

5. Add the chopped spinach to the skillet and cook until it wilts about 2-3 minutes.

6. In a bowl, combine the sautéed onion, garlic, and spinach with the chopped mushroom stems, cashews, and grated Parmesan cheese (if using). Mix well to combine.

7. Drizzle the remaining tablespoon of olive oil over the mushroom caps. Season them with salt and pepper.

8. Spoon the spinach and cashew mixture into each mushroom cap, pressing it down gently.

9. Place the stuffed mushrooms in the preheated oven and bake for about 20-25 minutes until the mushrooms are tender and the filling is golden brown.

10. After taking them out of the oven, give them some time to cool.

11. Garnish with fresh parsley if desired, and serve the stuffed Portobello mushrooms as a flavorful and satisfying main dish or appetizer.

Ingredients

- 2 large eggplants
- 2 red bell peppers
- 2 tablespoons olive oil
- 1 cup ricotta cheese (or vegan ricotta for a dairy-free option)
- 1/4 cup grated Parmesan cheese (optional)
- 2 tablespoons chopped fresh basil
- 2 cloves garlic, minced
- Salt and pepper to taste
- Tomato sauce for serving
- Fresh basil leaves for garnish (optional)

Instructions

1. Preheat the grill to medium heat.

2. Slice the eggplants lengthwise into thin strips, about 1/4-inch thick.

3. Cut the red bell peppers in half, remove the seeds and membranes, and flatten them.

4. Brush both sides of the eggplant slices and red pepper halves with olive oil.

5. Place the eggplant slices and red pepper halves on the grill. Cook for 3-4 minutes per side or until slightly charred and softened. After taking them off the grill, let them cool.

6. In a bowl, combine the ricotta cheese, grated Parmesan cheese (if using), chopped fresh basil, minced garlic, salt, and pepper. Mix well to combine.

7. Take one grilled eggplant slice and spread a thin layer of the ricotta mixture on top. Roll up the eggplant tightly and place it on a serving dish or baking dish, seam side down. Repeat with the remaining eggplant slices.

8. Once all the eggplant rolls are assembled, take a grilled red pepper half and place an eggplant roll inside. Roll up the red pepper tightly around the eggplant. Repeat with the remaining red pepper halves and eggplant rolls.

9. Place the filled red pepper and eggplant rolls on the grill for a few minutes to warm them through.

10. Remove from the grill and let them cool slightly before serving.

11. Serve the grilled eggplant and red pepper involtini with tomato sauce drizzled on top. Garnish with fresh basil leaves if desired.

CHAPTER 6

Side Dish Recipes

The diversity, flavor, and nutritional value of side dishes are important when putting together a balanced meal. Choosing kidney-friendly side dishes is crucial for people on a renal diet in order to maintain kidney health and general wellbeing.

When choosing side dishes, a renal diet focuses on controlling the intake of specific elements like sodium, potassium, and phosphorus, which can be difficult. However, with a little imagination and familiarity with kidney-friendly products, you can make scrumptious and filling side dishes that abide by dietary regulations.

This article will discuss a variety of side dish recipes created especially for a renal diet. These dishes will place an emphasis on healthy, fresh foods that are low in phosphorus, potassium, and salt while yet offering pleasing flavors.

These side dish dishes offer a variety of options to go with your main courses, from roasted veggies to savory grains, from fresh salads to warm casseroles. We can improve the flavor of these foods without using a lot of salt or items with a lot of potassium by adding herbs, spices, and other seasonings.

These side dish dishes will be a useful tool for anyone treating renal illness or just trying to maintain kidney health. They'll motivate you to prepare tasty, nutritious meals that are kind to your kidneys. By selecting healthy ingredients and using cooking methods that maintain nutritional content, you may make side dishes that support wellbeing and satisfaction.

So let's get started with these kidney-friendly side dish dishes and experience the delight of savory and nutritional options that will enhance your meals while promoting kidney health.

Ingredients

- 2 pounds of young potatoes, quartered or cut in half

- 2 tablespoons olive oil

- 3 cloves garlic, minced

- 1 tablespoon fresh rosemary, chopped

- 1 tablespoon fresh thyme leaves

- Salt and pepper to taste

Instructions

1. Preheat your oven to 425°F (220°C).
2. combine the halved or quartered baby potatoes, olive oil, minced garlic, chopped rosemary, and thyme leaves in a large mixing bowl.
3. Season with salt and pepper to taste, and toss well to ensure the potatoes are evenly coated with the oil and herbs.
4. Transfer the seasoned potatoes to a baking sheet, spreading them in a single layer.
5. Roast in the preheated oven for about 25-30 minutes, or until the potatoes are golden brown and crispy on the outside and tender on the inside. Stir the potatoes halfway through the cooking time to ensure even browning.
6. Once roasted, remove the potatoes from the oven and let them cool slightly before serving.
7. Transfer the garlic and herb-roasted potatoes to a serving dish and garnish with additional fresh herbs if desired.
8. Serve the roasted potatoes as a delicious and kidney-friendly side dish alongside your favourite protein or as part of a balanced meal.

Ingredients

- 1 bunch of asparagus spears, tough ends trimmed

- 2 tablespoons olive oil

- Zest of 1 lemon

- 2 tablespoons freshly squeezed lemon juice

- 1/4 cup grated Parmesan cheese

- Salt and pepper to taste

Instructions

1. Preheat your grill to medium-high heat.

2. combine the asparagus spears, olive oil, lemon zest, lemon juice, salt, and pepper in a shallow dish. Toss well to ensure the asparagus is evenly coated.

3. Place the asparagus spears on the preheated grill, perpendicular to the grates, to prevent them from falling through.

4. Grill the asparagus for about 5-7 minutes, turning occasionally or until they become tender and slightly charred.

5. remove the asparagus and transfer them to a serving platter once grilled.

6. Sprinkle the grated Parmesan cheese over the hot asparagus, allowing it to melt slightly.

7. Serve the grilled asparagus with lemon and Parmesan immediately as a flavorful and kidney-friendly side dish.

Ingredients

- 1 medium-sized butternut squash, peeled, seeded, and cubed

- 2 tablespoons olive oil

- 2 tablespoons pure maple syrup

- 1 teaspoon ground cinnamon

- Salt to taste

Instructions

1. Preheat your oven to 400°F (200°C) and line a baking sheet with parchment paper.

2. In a large bowl, combine the cubed butternut squash, olive oil, maple syrup, ground cinnamon, and a pinch of salt. Toss thoroughly to evenly coat the squash.

3. Transfer the seasoned butternut squash to the prepared baking sheet, spreading it in a single layer.

4. Bake in the preheated oven for about 25-30 minutes, or until the squash is tender and caramelized, turning once halfway through to ensure even cooking.

5. Once baked, remove the butternut squash from the oven and let it cool slightly before serving.

6. Transfer the baked butternut squash to a serving dish and sprinkle with an extra pinch of cinnamon if desired.

7. Serve the warm and comforting baked butternut squash with cinnamon and maple syrup as a flavorful and kidney-friendly side dish.

Ingredients

- 1 pound Brussels sprouts, trimmed and halved

- 2 tablespoons olive oil

- Salt and pepper to taste

- 1/2 cup pomegranate seeds

- 1/4 cup chopped pistachios

- Optional: balsamic glaze or reduction for drizzling

Instructions

1. Preheat your oven to 425°F (220°C) and line a baking sheet with parchment paper.

2. In a large bowl, toss the halved Brussels sprouts with olive oil, salt, and pepper until they are evenly coated.

3. Spread the Brussels sprouts in a single layer on the prepared baking sheet.

4. Roast in the preheated oven for about 20-25 minutes, or until the Brussels sprouts are golden brown and crispy, stirring once halfway through to ensure even browning.

5. Once roasted, remove the Brussels sprouts from the oven and let them cool slightly.

6. Transfer the roasted Brussels sprouts to a serving dish and sprinkle them with pomegranate seeds and chopped pistachios.

7. Optional: Drizzle the roasted Brussels sprouts with balsamic glaze or reduction for added flavour.

8. Serve the roasted Brussels sprouts with pomegranate and pistachios as a delicious and kidney-friendly side dish.

Ingredients

- 1 pound green beans, trimmed

- 2 tablespoons olive oil

- 2 cloves garlic, minced

- 1/4 cup sliced almonds

- Salt and pepper to taste

Instructions

1. Boil some salted water in a pot. Green beans should be crisp-tender after around 4-5 minutes of cooking after being added. Green beans should be drained and kept aside.

2. In a big skillet, warm the olive oil over medium heat. Sliced almonds and minced garlic are added to the skillet and cooked for 2 to 3 minutes, until the almonds are lightly toasted and the garlic is aromatic.

3. Add the cooked green beans to the skillet and toss them in the garlic and almond mixture until they are well coated. Sauté for 2-3 minutes, allowing the flavours to combine and the green beans to heat through.

4. Season with salt and pepper to taste, and toss the green beans once more to distribute the seasoning evenly.

5. Transfer the green beans with toasted almonds and garlic to a serving dish.

6. Serve the flavorful and kidney-friendly green beans as a nutritious side dish that pairs well with various main courses.

CHAPTER 7

Dessert Recipes

Even when on a renal diet, enjoying a sweet treat is something to be appreciated. A renal diet has particular restrictions, but there are still lots of delicious delicacies that may be enjoyed while keeping the kidneys healthy. Desserts may give a meal a satisfying and cozy ending. They are adaptable to a lifestyle that is beneficial to the kidneys.

Desserts should always be made using reduced salt, phosphorus, and potassium ingredients when following a renal diet. This can entail substituting items and watching portion quantities. But with a little imagination, you can make delicious treats that are good for your kidneys.

An assortment of dessert recipes that fit a renal diet will be covered in this guide. These dishes will include kidney-friendly components including fruits, dairy substitutes with low phosphorus content, and little to no additional sugar. We will discuss a variety of sweets that cater to various taste preferences, from zingy fruit salads to rich puddings.

You may prioritize your kidney health while still enjoying sweets by adhering to a renal diet. These dessert recipes will sate your sweet desire while also providing the flavors and nutrients that make sweets delightful. So let's explore desserts that are kind to kidneys and find delicious options you can enjoy guilt-free.

Ingredients

- 2 ripe avocados

- 1/4 cup unsweetened cocoa powder

- 1/4 cup agave nectar or maple syrup

- 1/4 cup plant-based milk (such as almond or coconut milk)

- 1 teaspoon vanilla extract

- Optional toppings: sliced strawberries, chopped nuts, shredded coconut

Instructions

1. Remove the pits from the avocados by cutting them in half, then scoop the flesh into a food processor or blender.

2. Add cocoa powder, maple syrup, agave nectar, plant-based milk, and vanilla extract to the blender.

3. Blend all items until they are creamy and smooth. Stop and scrape down the sides of the blender to ensure everything is well incorporated.

4. Taste the mixture and adjust the sweetness if desired by adding more maple syrup or agave nectar.

5. Transfer the pudding to serving bowls or glasses once it reaches a smooth consistency.

6. Cover the bowls with plastic wrap or place the glasses in the refrigerator for 1-2 hours to chill and set.

7. When ready to serve, remove the pudding from the refrigerator and garnish with sliced strawberries, chopped nuts, or shredded coconut if desired.

8. Enjoy the creamy, decadent vegan chocolate avocado pudding as a kidney-friendly dessert.

Strawberry and Rhubarb Crumble

Ingredients

- 2 cups strawberries, hulled and sliced

- 2 cups rhubarb, diced

- 1/4 cup granulated sugar (or sugar substitute, if preferred)

- 1 tablespoon cornstarch

- 1 teaspoon lemon juice

- 1 cup rolled oats

- 1/2 cup almond flour

- 1/4 cup chopped walnuts

- 1/4 cup melted coconut oil

- 2 tablespoons maple syrup or agave nectar

- 1/2 teaspoon cinnamon

- Pinch of salt

Instructions

1. Preheat your oven to 350°F (175°C).

2. combine the strawberries, rhubarb, granulated sugar (or sugar substitute), cornstarch, and lemon juice in a mixing bowl. Stir well until the fruit is coated and the sugar is dissolved. Let the mixture sit for about 10 minutes to release some juices.

3. In a separate bowl, prepare the crumble topping by combining the rolled oats, almond flour, chopped walnuts, melted coconut oil, maple syrup or agave nectar, cinnamon, and a pinch of salt. Mix until the components are thoroughly incorporated and take on a crumbly consistency.

4. Transfer the strawberry and rhubarb mixture to a baking dish or individual ramekins.

5. Sprinkle the crumble topping evenly over the fruit mixture, covering it completely.

6. Place the baking dish or ramekins in the oven and bake for about 30-35 minutes, or until the fruit is bubbly and the crumble topping is golden brown.

7. Before serving, take it out of the oven and allow it to cool for a while..

8. Serve the strawberry and rhubarb crumble warm or at room temperature. It pairs well with a scoop of vanilla ice cream or a dollop of whipped cream if desired.

Banana Oat Cookies

Ingredients

- 2 ripe bananas, mashed

- 1 cup rolled oats

- One-fourth cup of almond or peanut butter

- Optional: 1/4 cup raisins or chopped dried fruit

- 1 tablespoon maple syrup or honey

- 1/2 teaspoon vanilla extract

- 1/2 teaspoon cinnamon

- Pinch of salt

Instructions

1. Set a baking sheet on your oven's 350°F (175°C) rack and preheat the oven.

2. In a mixing bowl, combine the mashed bananas, rolled oats, almond butter or peanut butter, raisins or dried fruit (if using), maple syrup or honey, vanilla extract, cinnamon, and a pinch of salt. Stir everything up thoroughly until well-combined.

3. Let the mixture sit for about 10 minutes, allowing the oats to absorb moisture and soften.

4. Using a spoon or your hands, scoop portions of the cookie mixture and shape them into round cookie shapes. Place them on the prepared baking sheet, leaving a little space between each cookie.

5. Flatten the cookies slightly with a spoon or your fingers to ensure even baking.

6. Bake the cookies in the oven for about 12-15 minutes or until golden brown around the edges.

7. Remove the baking sheet from the oven and let the cookies cool for a few minutes before transferring them to a wire rack to cool completely.

8. Once the cookies have cooled, they are ready to enjoy. Any leftovers should be kept in an airtight container.

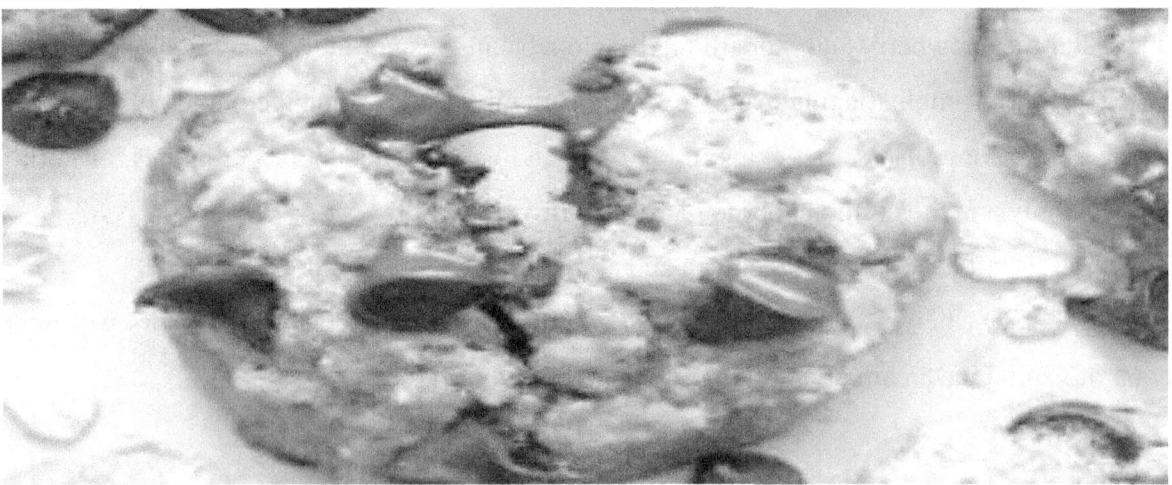

Vegan Chocolate Chip Blondies

Ingredients

- 1 cup all-purpose flour
- 1/2 cup almond flour
- 1/2 cup coconut sugar
- 1/2 cup vegan butter, melted
- A quarter cup of agave nectar or maple syrup
- 1/4 cup plant-based milk (such as almond or soy milk)
- 1 teaspoon vanilla extract
- 1/2 teaspoon baking powder
- 1/4 teaspoon salt
- 1/2 cup vegan chocolate chips

Instructions

1. Preheat your oven to 350°F (175°C) and line a baking dish with parchment paper.

2. In a mixing bowl, combine the all-purpose flour, almond flour, coconut sugar, baking powder, and salt. Stir well to ensure the dry ingredients are evenly mixed.

3. In a separate bowl, whisk together the melted vegan butter, maple syrup or agave nectar, plant-based milk, and vanilla extract until well combined.

4. Pour the wet ingredients into the bowl of dry ingredients and mix until a thick batter forms.

5. Fold in the vegan chocolate chips, reserving a few for sprinkling on top.

6. Transfer the batter to the lined baking dish, spreading it evenly with a spatula.

7. Sprinkle the remaining chocolate chips on top of the batter.

8. Bake in the preheated oven for about 25-30 minutes, or until the blondies are golden brown around the edges and a toothpick inserted into the centre comes out with a few moist crumbs.

9. Remove the baking dish from the oven and let the blondies cool completely before cutting them into squares.

10. Serve and enjoy these vegan chocolate chip blondies as a delicious and satisfying treat.

Ingredients

- 4 medium-sized apples (such as Granny Smith or Honeycrisp)
- 2 tablespoons of maple syrup
- 1 tablespoon of melted butter (or coconut oil for a vegan option)
- 1 teaspoon of ground cinnamon
- 1/4 cup of chopped nuts (such as walnuts or pecans)
- Optional toppings: whipped cream, vanilla ice cream, or Greek yogurt

Instructions

1. Preheat your oven to 375°F (190°C).

2. Start by washing the apples thoroughly and patting them dry. Remove the core of each apple using an apple corer or a sharp knife, making sure to leave the bottom intact. This will create a small cavity for the filling.

3. In a small bowl, mix together the maple syrup, melted butter (or coconut oil), and ground cinnamon until well combined.

4. Place the apples in a baking dish or on a baking sheet lined with parchment paper.

5. Drizzle the maple syrup mixture evenly over each apple, making sure to coat the inside as well.

6. Sprinkle the chopped nuts over the top of the apples, distributing them evenly among the cavities.

7. Place the baking dish or sheet in the preheated oven and bake for approximately 25-30 minutes, or until the apples are tender when pierced with a fork. The baking time may vary depending on the size and variety of the apples.

8. Once baked, remove the apples from the oven and let them cool for a few minutes before serving.

9. You can serve the baked apples as they are or with optional toppings such as whipped cream, vanilla ice cream, or Greek yogurt. The choice is yours!

10. Enjoy your delicious Baked Apples with Cinnamon and Maple Syrup!

CONCLUSION

In conclusion, following a renal diet doesn't mean sacrificing the pleasure of enjoying tasty meals and desserts. By making mindful choices and incorporating kidney-friendly ingredients, it is possible to create various delicious dishes that align with renal health recommendations.

Throughout this guide, we have explored a range of recipes that cater to different dietary needs and preferences while prioritizing kidney health. From breakfast options like Sweet Potato and Spinach Breakfast Skillet to appetizers like Baked Sweet Potato Fries with Cilantro Lime Dip and desserts like Vegan Chocolate Avocado Pudding, we have covered a diverse selection of recipes. These recipes provide nourishment while limiting the strain on the kidneys by focusing on low-sodium, low-phosphorus, and low-potassium ingredients. It's essential to consult with a healthcare professional or registered dietitian to determine specific dietary requirements and portion sizes that best suit individual needs.

By embracing the creativity and versatility of ingredients, one can still enjoy a flavorful and satisfying culinary experience. Whether it's the vibrant colours of salads or the comforting indulgence of desserts, the recipes presented in this guide offer kidney-friendly and delicious options.

Remember, a renal diet supports kidney health and manages certain conditions. It is essential to maintain a balanced approach and prioritize overall well-being. Enjoy these recipes as part of a holistic approach to a healthy lifestyle, including regular exercise, hydration, and adherence to any prescribed medications.

Here's to a flavorful and fulfilling journey in exploring renal-friendly recipes that bring joy while nurturing your kidney health.

APPENDIX

Day 1

- Breakfast: Quinoa Porridge with Mixed Berries

- Snack: Raw Veggie Sticks with Hummus

- Lunch: Tuna Salad Lettuce Wraps with Roasted Vegetables

- Snack: Baked Sweet Potato Fries with Cilantro Lime Dip

- Dinner: Grilled Chicken with Lemon Herb Sauce, Roasted Asparagus, and Brown Rice

Day 2

- Breakfast: Vegan Blueberry Pancakes with Almond Butter

- Snack: Apple Slices with Almond Butter

- Lunch: Grilled Shrimp Skewers with Grilled Vegetables and Brown Rice

- Snack: Raw Nuts

- Dinner: Vegetable and Bean Chili with Avocado

Day 3

- Breakfast: Sweet Potato and Spinach Breakfast Skillet

- Snack: Fresh Fruit Salad

- Lunch: Chicken Caesar Salad with Low-Sodium Dressing

- Snack: Baked Apple Chips

- Dinner: Grilled Salmon with Mango Salsa, Roasted Vegetables, and Quinoa

Day 4

- Breakfast: Chia Seed Pudding with Berries

- Snack: Baked Veggie Chips

- Lunch: Tofu Stir Fry with Brown Rice and Vegetables

- Snack: Raw Veggie Sticks with Hummus

- Dinner: Turkey Meatballs with Marinara Sauce, Zucchini Noodles, and Side Salad

Day 5

- Breakfast: Almond Butter and Banana Smoothie

- Snack: Raw Nuts

- Lunch: Grilled Chicken Caesar Salad with Low-Sodium Dressing

- Snack: Roasted Chickpeas

- Dinner: Baked Cod with Lemon and Herbs, Roasted Vegetables, and Brown Rice

Day 6

- Breakfast: Vegan Banana Oat Cookies with Fresh Berries

- Snack: Baked Sweet Potato Fries with Cilantro Lime Dip

- Lunch: Quinoa and Kale Salad with Cranberries and Almonds

- Snack: Fresh Fruit Salad

- Dinner: Grilled Steak with Mushroom Sauce, Roasted Asparagus, and Quinoa

Day 7

- Breakfast: Tofu Scramble with Veggies

- Snack: Apple Slices with Almond Butter

- Lunch: Roasted Red Pepper Hummus with Raw Veggie Sticks

- Snack: Raw Nuts

- Dinner: Grilled Chicken Skewers with Grilled Vegetables and Brown Rice

Day 8

- Breakfast: Vegan Chocolate Avocado Pudding

- Snack: Raw Veggie Sticks with Hummus

- Lunch: Grilled Shrimp Salad with Low-Sodium Dressing

- Snack: Baked Apple Chips

- Dinner: Vegetable Curry with Brown Rice

- Breakfast: Baked Apples with Cinnamon and Maple Syrup

- Snack: Fresh Fruit Salad

- Lunch: Tuna Salad Lettuce Wraps with Roasted Vegetables

- Snack: Raw Nuts

- Dinner: Grilled Salmon with Lemon Herb Sauce, Roasted Vegetables, and Quinoa

- Breakfast: Vegan Blueberry Pancakes with Almond Butter

- Snack: Raw Veggie Sticks with Hummus

- Lunch: Chicken Caesar Salad with Low-Sodium Dressing

- Snack: Baked Sweet Potato Fries with Cilantro Lime Dip

- Dinner: Grilled Chicken with Mango Salsa, Roasted Vegetables, and Brown Rice

- Breakfast: Sweet Potato and Spinach Breakfast Skillet

- Snack: Raw Nuts

- Lunch: Grilled Shrimp Skewers with Quinoa and Grilled Vegetables

- Snack: Fresh Fruit Salad

- Dinner: Vegetable and Bean Chili with Avocado

- Breakfast: Chia Seed Pudding with Berries

- Snack: Baked Veggie Chips

- Lunch: Tofu Stir Fry with Brown Rice and Vegetables

- Snack: Raw Veggie Sticks with Hummus

- Dinner: Baked Cod with Lemon and Herbs, Roasted Vegetables, and Quinoa

- Breakfast: Almond Butter and Banana Smoothie

- Snack: Raw Nuts

- Lunch: Grilled Chicken Caesar Salad with Low-Sodium Dressing

- Snack: Roasted Chickpeas

- Dinner: Turkey Meatballs with Marinara Sauce, Zucchini Noodles, and Side Salad

Day 14

- Breakfast: Vegan Banana Oat Cookies with Fresh Berries

- Snack: Baked Sweet Potato Fries with Cilantro Lime Dip

- Lunch: Quinoa and Kale Salad with Cranberries and Almonds

- Snack: Fresh Fruit Salad

- Dinner: Grilled Steak with Mushroom Sauce, Roasted Asparagus, and Quinoa

Made in United States
North Haven, CT
12 September 2023

41474494R00037